WHO'S RUNNING THIS TOWN, ANYWAY?

NEW DIMENSIONS OF LOCAL GOVERNMENT LEADERSHIP

John C. Buechner, Ph.D.

iUniverse, Inc.
New York   Bloomington

Who's Running This Town, Anyway?
New Dimensions of Local Government Leadership

Copyright © 2008 by John C. Buechner

All rights reserved. No part of this book may be used or reproduced by any means, graphic, electronic, or mechanical, including photocopying, recording, taping or by any information storage retrieval system without the written permission of the publisher except in the case of brief quotations embodied in critical articles and reviews.

The views expressed in this work are solely those of the author and do not necessarily reflect the views of the publisher, and the publisher hereby disclaims any responsibility for them.
iUniverse books may be ordered through booksellers or by contacting:

iUniverse
1663 Liberty Drive
Bloomington, IN 47403
www.iuniverse.com
1-800-Authors (1-800-288-4677)

Because of the dynamic nature of the Internet, any Web addresses or links contained in this book may have changed since publication and may no longer be valid. The views expressed in this work are solely those of the author and do not necessarily reflect the views of the publisher, and the publisher hereby disclaims any responsibility for them.

ISBN: 978-0-595-51646-9 (pbk)
ISBN: 978-0-595-61978-8 (ebk)

Printed in the United States of America

Contents

ACKNOWLEDGMENTS	vi
INTRODUCTION	vii
THE UNIQUENESS OF LOCAL GOVERNMENT POLITICS	1
Characteristics of Council Life	2
Tension Points	3
Formal and Informal Roles	8
The Mayor	11
The Changing Landscape	13
OUTSIDE-IN CULTURAL CHANGES	15
Major Personal, Work, and Group Adjustments	16
Rapidly Changing Technological Dimensions	17
Substantial Growth in Numbers and Activities of Governments	20
Demographic Changes	24
THE NEED FOR NEW AND DIFFERENT LEADERSHIP PARADIGMS	27
A Typology of Council Leaders	28
The Leadership Paradigm Shift	31
The Characteristics and Traits of a 21st Century Renaissance Leader	33
CONCLUSION	38
TITLES FOR THE BOOKSHELF OF EVERY LOCAL OFFICIAL	41
ABOUT THE AUTHOR	44

ACKNOWLEDGMENTS

I want to thank Robert Buechner (retired city manager), Chris Cameron (mayor of Lafayette, Colorado), Gary Klaphake (city administrator of Lafayette, Colorado), Jeffrey A. Roberts (editing consultant), Ronald Secrist (retired city manager), and many other public officials and students over the past 45 years. I also want to thank many friends and members of my family, especially Mary Buechner Fetterly.

INTRODUCTION

City councils wrestle with increasingly longer and more complex agenda items. They hear from citizens who demand quality municipal services and expect problems to be solved immediately. They may be frustrated in their inability to find new revenue sources to meet existing needs and plan for the future at the same time. American cities and towns in the 21st century face a wide spectrum of issues and problems, many of which are the consequences of decisions made by other levels of government. Moreover, city charter or statutory provisions often limit the degree to which councils can respond to issues. Finally, the population is changing in its makeup, how it views government, and what it expects from government.

Trying to become more responsive and efficient, local governments have experimented with various organizational schemes: the council-manager plan, direct election of the mayor, consolidation of governments, changing how council members are elected, and others. It is unlikely that some new and different form of local government will be invented. Rather, there will be episodic, band-aid proposals for reorganizing city governments. Some may lead to good outcomes and some may result in less effectiveness.

The purpose of this little book is not to prophesize that the sky is falling on cities and towns or to suggest that those holding public office lack commitment and dedication in their representative roles. It is argued here that city and town councils

John C. Buechner

are generally locked into governance structures that restrict them from being more effective. Additionally, while councils are bombarded with demands, requests, and even threats, they are often unable – through no fault of their own – to satisfy all constituencies. The fundamental premise is this: For councils to fulfill their roles more effectively in today's world and that of tomorrow requires a transformation not of the structure of governance but of a government's culture, using different and possibly new leadership styles. While city and town councils will continue to function in already established forms of government, they must change rigid habits, arrangements, and thoughts. I call this the development of an *outside-in* culture, one that discards unnecessary processes, procedures, and structures; allows extensive probing and questioning of premises and arrangements; and avoids the status quo in making decisions. This approach necessarily requires councils to thoroughly examine their formal legal roles as well as their informal roles. Councils in large and small towns must comprehend the changing nature of society beyond their city limits and how these changes influence citizen behavior within their communities. An outside-in culture also suggests the need to elect and appoint people who, for want of a better word, exhibit *renaissance* leadership skills and talents.

In the next few pages it is hoped the reader will be prompted to engage in in-depth discussions about councils and their behavior. There is no intent here to write a history of the American city, neither to prepare a college or university text nor to propose this as a primer on local government. And by no means is this book written to serve as *the* book for local government problem solving. No doubt councils, mayors, and administrators will continue to grapple with the usual issues, such as street repairs, crime and fire prevention, zoning and planning, and all that appropriately falls within the domain of local government control and responsibility. But a new leadership paradigm is needed to guide those councils, mayors, and administrators as they set direction and make governmental decisions. As problems and issues become more pronounced, the community reaction to the behavior of councils might lead to the citizen mantra of "Who's Running This Town, Anyway?"* Most council members will answer, "We are!" But the world of local government changes so rapidly that it is difficult, if not almost impossible, to meet community needs and wants resulting from the effects of urban life. Effective leadership is what cities and towns need most.

John C. Buechner

*A word of attribution. Years ago, I recall learning about a book by Ritchie P. Lowry, *Who's Running This Town? Community Leadership and Social Change* (Harper & Row publishers, 1962). I have not used Lowry's book in this work, but I have copied, in part, his book title. Lowry's book is out of print, but copies may be secured on Amazon.com. I recommend it as a sociologist's approach to community leadership.

THE UNIQUENESS OF LOCAL GOVERNMENT POLITICS

"Serving on a city council can be a headache, but democracy is based on the assumption that some people are willing to endure headaches."

– The author

Why do people run for city council? There are myriad possible motivations – devotion to community, revenge, political loyalties, self fulfillment, the notion it could be a stepping stone to higher political office, or any combination of these and other factors. In some communities candidates for council emerge at the behest of friends, work associates, interest groups, or political party loyalists. Unlike with other elective offices, tenure on a city council is usually an appendage to one's vocation. It is safe to say that the allure of council service may not be fully grasped until well after one's term of office has begun. Whatever the underlying reasons for seeking council office, most council members' original perceptions about council life change as they become seasoned on the job. As one pundit observed, "Service on a city council acts as a great civilizer for most individuals."

John C. Buechner

CHARACTERISTICS OF COUNCIL LIFE

Although one cannot generalize about motivations for seeking election to councils, there are some dominant characteristics that help define the uniqueness of council life: amateurism, geographic proximity, differences in the roles of local government officials, and the decision-making process.

A standard definition of *amateurs* suggests that they are dabblers, people who participate but not with the desire for long-term service. Amateurs do not lack talent or commitment or the ability to grasp their roles. Rather, it is presumed that those elected to town or city councils are not so-called professional politicians but instead are concerned citizens serving a representative function.

It has been said that a council member's constituents are omnipresent. A goldfish bowl existence means that council members suffer (or succeed) from geographic proximity to the community. No matter where a council member goes – the grocery, church, a cocktail party, work, or even a casual neighborhood stroll – he or she is fair game for constituent conversation, criticism, and even personal requests for city action or attention. Unlike their counterparts in elective office at the state or federal level, council members cannot escape public scrutiny behind the two-party system, a two-house legislative assembly, geographical distance from constituents back home, or a complicated and large bureaucracy. Like it or not, council members are highly visible in a multitude of venues and, consequently, they also are highly vulnerable to community criticism. As one councilman said, "The day before I was elected those who I talked with referred to themselves as citizens; the day after I was elected the same people referred to themselves as taxpayers."

It is sometimes difficult for a council member to understand his or her role. Often, newly elected council members believe they have a clear-cut mandate from voters to make various changes in the way their local governments make decisions. Either by statute or local charter, councils have a policy-making role rather than an administrative one. Newly elected councils often fail to make the necessary distinctions between making public policy and administering public policy. In addition, there is often a misguided notion that local government policies are one-time events, pieces of paper that stand in perpetuity, easily retrieved from a shelf of documents in city hall whenever a decision is to be made. In reality, policy making is an on-going process consisting of repeals of, or amendments to, decisions made in the course of city business. This does not mean new and innovative policies are prohibited. But once enacted, policies are implemented by the city manager or others charged with administration.

Similarly, the decision-making process is often misunderstood. Political scientist Norton Long characterized it as "disjointed incrementalism" or "the science of muddling through." Most decisions are made incrementally and much depends on existing, as well as unforeseen, circumstances facing the community. Thus, councils generally make decisions as issues and problems emerge. While efforts are made to make the *right* decisions, council decision making often is complicated by value judgments, emotions, and public reactions. While "muddling through" should not be embraced as an underlying *modus operandi*, councils should accept that a large degree of the decision process is indeed incremental.

Tension Points

There are at least five discernible tension points that may occur separately or simultaneously in the life of a council member: the media, the public at large or segments of the community, council colleagues, the administrative staff, and work or personal relationships.

In general, reporters are eager to discover and report about city issues and how members of council react to them and vote on them. The print media will not report verbatim everything said about an agenda item. They will, however, look for statements by council members that may not have been intended for publication. Members of councils should weigh carefully what they say if they wish to avoid reading their words in the next edition of a newspaper. It is no secret, however, that some members of council purposely make statements, often written in advance, hoping that their comments will indeed appear in the print media. Overuse of this practice can be problematic; council colleagues might complain about being caught off guard, for instance. The televising of council meetings in many communities has created another tension point. Though intended to facilitate communication between those who govern and the public, it may also have negative consequences. In most cities and towns, televised meetings are live broadcasts with no interpreter to describe what is happening. To the casual observer, council meetings may seem awkward, lacking in decorum or, at times, non-productive. Members of council need to realize that unorthodox body language, confusing or silly comments, or inarticulateness can easily be seen by viewers. Some public television stations repeat council sessions between regularly scheduled meetings, allowing even greater public review of the council at work. Some council members see the televising of meetings not so much as a tension point but as an opportunity to satisfy their own ego needs regardless of the issue at hand.

Elected representatives should expect conflict at times between themselves and segments of the public. Most citizens are neutral about city government issues until they are disadvantaged or inconvenienced because of city actions or inactions. When potholes are not repaired, when leash laws are not enforced, when zoning changes are considered, or any number of issues surface, citizens individually or in groups expect the council to act. Depending on the nature of an issue, public involvement in the governing process can be benign or, in the extreme, call for the recall or dismissal of officials. One can argue that this form of tension comes with the territory – councils are expected to address thorny and complex issues. Dilatory or casual reaction to public concerns can easily shift the debate away from the substance of an issue to a larger discussion about the overall effectiveness of the city council. Clearly, councils should be sincere listeners to public opinion while focusing first on the facts of a situation, then on problem-solving methods, a review of the city's major goals, and a reexamination of the community's core values. While tensions between the council and the public cannot be totally eliminated, effective council behavior can demonstrate that every effort is being made to address and resolve public concerns.

While responsiveness to public questions, requests, and demands should be a high agenda item for councils, it may be too late and too little in coming. Councils often think a public hearing is an adequate way to respond to the public. But if not handled correctly, public hearings can have less value than having none at all. Councils should be prepared to act in some way in response to comments offered in public hearings. To do otherwise will simply exacerbate an issue and reinforce what might already be negative public perceptions about the council's ability to resolve problems. The public usually is eager to hear how things will be handled and what structure is in place for closure on issues. If the council appears to be at a loss as to how it plans to resolve an issue, those attending a hearing will undoubtedly focus on the council's behavior more than on the pros and cons of the question. Depending on the volatility of an issue, a public hearing often is not enough to put it to rest.

Public reaction to local government activities has taken on new and different forms. Neighborhood groups and associations often focus on specific problems – such as crime, street repair, or traffic controls – of particular interest to a specific geographical area. Mobilization of citizen action in neighborhoods has meant that councils, whether elected by districts or at large, must pay attention to distinct segments of the community. Ironically, modern city planning has indirectly fostered cohesive neighborhood interaction and detachment from other areas of the community. While one could argue this has a beneficial side, it may well make it more difficult to address citywide problems. Coupled with neighborhood activities is the growth of printed media attention to specific neighborhoods. Free weekly newspapers often focus on localized topics. Blogging also allows easy citizen participation in a way that cuts across geographic, gender, occupational, and political lines. There are more avenues for generating public awareness, understanding, and input than ever before. Individuals can pick and choose the format for their participation and easily enlist others as supporters.

Tension points between members of city councils can cause breakdowns in the decision-making process, sometimes of such a magnitude that reconciliation is virtually impossible. While controversy, disagreement, and debate are integral parts of legislative behavior, personal attacks, insults, and petty arguments should not be the norm. The actions of council cliques or blocs of members can make council meetings seem more like sideshows rather than examples of sound, representative government. The seasoned council member learns to avoid *ad hominem* arguments and tries to keep differences at substantive levels. Continued and increased personal arguments between members inevitably leads to ineffective decision making, unnecessary media attention and, in some cases, changes in administrative staff and those in leadership positions.

Although most city councils, particularly those under the council-manager plan, are elected on non-partisan ballots, ideological tension points arise at times. In some cities and towns non-partisanship is given only lip service and the political party affiliations of candidates, while not identified on a ballot, are well known to voters. A kind of latent partisanship can surface if these circumstances arise, making the task of reaching consensus on purely local matters difficult. Fiorello H. LaGuardia, mayor of New York City in the 1930s and 1940s, once remarked, "There is no Democratic or Republican way of cleaning the streets." Partisanship often surfaces when extraneous agenda items, such as resolutions on U.S. military involvements or those addressing topics that can only be resolved at other levels of government, direct council attention away from purely local concerns.

The home and workplace also can be sources of stress for council members. It is not easy to separate the role of elected representative from other roles. Telephone calls, faxes, cell phone use, late meetings, special study sessions – all designed to facilitate the council process – may have negative consequences by intruding on family, work, or social life. There are situations, for example, where a business has been adversely affected because of a council member's vote or series of votes. Family members often are put in the awkward position of having to support or defend a council action even though they are not knowledgeable about the nuances underlying the decision process.

The relationship between the administrative staff and council also may be tense. The equation for the council-manager plan is on the one hand simple and on the other complex. Councils are to set direction and adopt policies governing the community while administrators are professionals given the task of implementing the policies. In many situations, however, these roles become blurred and guidelines for executing policies are vague or unclear. Councils sometimes attempt to administer as well as set policies, and the intent of policies may be lost. Professional staffs usually have information on a day-to-day basis and, at times, this threatens council members who see and hear the recommendations for policy action. There is always a question of how much information and backup material council members should get before decisions are made. They may feel like there is either too much information to absorb or not enough. Staff professionals are obligated to respond to council inquiries and recommend actions. Some councils believe their proper roles should be adversarial or that of watchdogs vis-à-vis the administrative staff. Councils, however, possess ultimate decision-making authority based on sound recommendations. There is a temptation to become too involved in the administrative side of the equation while neglecting the intent of the policy under consideration. Such behavior can actually undermine staff and send mixed messages to the public about differentiated and clearly defined roles. It is incumbent upon council members to question, reflect, analyze, and critique recommendations brought before them. Similarly, it is incumbent upon the administration to set forth recommendations with appropriate support data so that sound policies are executed. Keeping respective roles in focus goes a long way toward minimizing council-staff tensions. When roles become blurred any number of consequences can occur – professional staff leave employment, there are calls for a new form of government or charter or statutory changes, council members resign or do not seek reelection, or there is increased public disenchantment with city affairs.

Formal and Informal Roles

Certain roles and responsibilities must be fulfilled by councils as set forth by charter, ordinance, statute, or state constitution. The extent and depth to which these formal roles are executed may be determined by population size, socio-economic characteristics, and other factors. In essence, the formal or legally empowered roles include financier, employer, purchaser, and lawmaker. In many instances councils also perform quasi-judicial functions, such as sitting as an urban renewal authority or liquor licensing board.

There is an old saying, "Money isn't everything, but it certainly beats whatever is in second place!" Councils have the task of setting annual budgets and most have the authority to set fees and taxes and make long-range bonding commitments. Of course, nobody pickets city hall for higher taxes. Councils have the ongoing dilemma of deciding, both in the short and long terms, how to pay for government services and community needs and wants.

While administrators are responsible for employing and removing employees, councils adopt policies such as classification and compensation plans and affirmative action programs, and they approve employee union contracts. Who is accountable for employing individuals is usually spelled out, but the overall responsibility for a community's employment practices rests with the council.

Similarly, councils are ultimately responsible for the purchase of land or major services. The council enacts ordinances governing bidding procedures and establishing ceilings on spending. In some instances the purchasing role may conflict with other priorities already in place. Expensive purchases, such as a new fire truck or snow plow, may lead to a council conflict over the need for the expenditure and the use of available dollars that could be spent on something else.

Fulfilling the role of lawmaker places the council in the position of having to draw the line between restraint and liberty. Council members often have difficulty appreciating this role because of a variety of inhibiting factors. Lawmaking can be frustrating because of pending or projected litigation and rules and regulations – state or federal – that may prohibit new laws. The successful initiation and passage of local laws is probably the most difficult of a council's formal roles.

How well informal, non-legal, or attendant roles are played usually determines whether a council member is effective in carrying out his or her formal responsibilities. At least three informal roles can be identified: mediator and clarifier, listener and consensus builder, and leader.

Members of a council have the opportunity to be mediators and clarifiers in a number of ways. Political scientist Arthur W. Bromage referred to this role as a "political brokerage" function. It is a perfectly appropriate role so long as the great game of city politics is played cleanly. Seasoned council members can help settle disputes between members and between the council and others, such as public groups or the administrative staff.

Disagreements often are caused by a lack of factual information or a miscommunication. In a clarifying or mediating role, a member of council can help reduce conflict, help manage conflict, and help others focus on issues at hand. In short, mediating and clarifying should become a conscious practice when formal roles are carried out. Clearly, one must also learn when not to mediate – how to identify and avoid the gray areas between honest and open mediation and when mediation can exacerbate rather than make a situation less difficult than it should be.

If there is any single area where council members can make mistakes it is not learning to be good listeners and consensus builders. Newly elected council members often believe that their election was in some way a mandate to opine on every issue. Nothing could be further from the truth. By avoiding the listening role, members of council often not only lose their effectiveness but rapidly are perceived as having predetermined opinions not necessarily based on facts. An equally bad problem exists when council members listen only to those who have easy access to them and who only reinforce their preconceived opinions. They should listen to critics as well as those in agreement. Moreover, seeking views and opinions from colleagues establishes the opportunity for consensus building rather than an equation that puts individuals in a *for* or *against* position. Finally, sometimes people just want the opportunity to talk to a public official. Not every conversation has to end in an action or solution to a problem.

Leadership is an elusive term, often wrongly ascribed only to those holding a title, such as city manager or mayor. Individual council members also should be leaders. When debate falters or the focus is blurred, any member of council can help fill the leadership void by influencing and persuading colleagues. This does not mean that individuals can assume an authoritative role or go beyond the boundaries of decorum. Rather, the elected representative can help direct discussion, reduce dissension, and avoid dilatory activity. Leadership is everyone's informal role if a council is to effectively make decisions.

There is no one best way to lead and there may be situations where overt leadership is not appropriate. The seasoned council member is able, through listening and other informal roles, to discern when a situation demands strong individual leadership. All too often, however, some council members believe they are showing leadership by taking action on an item or set of items. Mere voting does not necessarily equal leadership. Indeed, a conclusion to a debate or discussion does not, in and by itself, mean that the council was leading. The opposite may be true. Some city councils may be so lacking in leadership they can best be described as maintenance or caretaker bodies. When, over time, a council or a council member neglects the leadership role one thing is certain to follow – someone or some group will emerge to fill the void.

THE MAYOR

To become the mayor of a city or town, one must first be elected to the office – by the public directly or the council itself. The governmental structure of the city or town determines how the mayor is selected. Some cities and towns are governed by a mayor and a manager, some by a weak mayor and council, some by a strong mayor and council, and some by a chief administrative officer under the mayor and a council. The terms *strong* and *weak* do not suggest individuals holding these positions lack personal fortitude; rather, the powers and authorities given to these positions vary across a wide spectrum.

In most cities and towns, the mayor serves as chair of the council and ceremonial or titular head of the community. Under the council-manager plan, mayors are generally elected from the council membership and are, in fact, one among equals on the council. One should not minimize the title and ceremonial attributes of the mayor, however. The public perceives of the mayor, rightfully or wrongly, as the primary spokesperson for the city government, and mayors often exercise considerable community influence because of the title of the office. Obviously, the mayor must learn to differentiate when he or she is speaking on behalf of the entire council or as one of the council, especially when he or she has been elected from within the council. Even if the mayor is elected directly by the public, his or her legal authority may be no greater than other members of the council.

Still, people often turn to the mayor to bring issues to the attention of the city government. The seasoned mayor knows how to behave in this role so that others, such as the city administration and members of council, are not upstaged or caught by surprise by new or distressing information.

Most people elected to a council and/or to the position of mayor are thrust into a new and, at times, bewildering environment. Although some have served on community boards and commissions, council life is not the same. New issues, public scrutiny, tensions, and the knowledge that, in President Truman's words, "The buck stops here," add a heavy dimension to the role. City council members are asked to make decisions and lead, but frequently the environment is not what they expected and the relationships are not as collegial as anticipated. The seasoned council member does not violate the 11th commandment of public life – "Thou shall not wing it!" Rather, the seasoned council person learns to understand the formal roles and how to perform the informal roles. He or she does the necessary homework on problems and issues rather than hastily making decisions, is discerning in offering viewpoints, learns which issues are more important than others, and respects the need to be responsive as an elected representative.

All members of council reach an initial threshold of survival when they either become seasoned or not. When this occurs varies from person to person and community to community, but most council members know when it exists. Seniority is really not the same as reaching the so-called threshold. It is more or less a framework in which the council member functions differently than first exhibited. Matriculation into the seasoned class does not happen to everyone and is not taught in a formal way. Those who do not enter the initial survival stage often tire of their roles in government, fail in reelection bids, become disenchanted with the process and their colleagues, or all or any combination of the above. The amount of time and energy needed to serve on a council often discourages men and women from seeking election in the first place. In Colorado, 39 local elections were canceled in 2008 because of a lack of candidates or ballot measures. In 2006, 48 elections in Colorado were called off.

THE CHANGING LANDSCAPE

Reviewing how the urban landscape changed in the 20th century is a huge task. Major American cities endured large out-migrations to suburbs, economic downturns, housing crises, and much more. Local governments in rural communities faced declining populations, agricultural financial upheavals, and citizen demands for more and better basic services. The most populated communities in some rural areas had problems similar to those of large urban centers with just differences in degree, not in kind.

But near the end of the century, there was "a turnaround in the fortunes of urban America," observes Richard Florida (*The Rise of the Creative Class*, Basic Books, 2002). Professor Florida cites various forces that have brought people and economic activity back to urban areas, including reduced crime rates, technological innovations, and demographic changes.

In both urban and rural communities, those elected and appointed to make decisions are often advised by consultants to "think outside the box" while working to resolve current issues and simultaneously plan for the effects of a changing local government landscape. But in many instances, the decision makers cannot accurately describe what box they are currently in.

John C. Buechner

It is difficult for them to see how the changing landscape should affect their day-to-day and week-to-week actions.

Before a new leadership paradigm can emerge, local officials must embrace the outside-in culture previously described in this book. Changes resulting from factors outside a community necessitate not only an enlightened awareness of such changes, but the need to make the dynamics of these changes an integral part of the conduct of local government.

OUTSIDE-IN CULTURAL CHANGES

"I'm tired of hearing it said that democracy doesn't work. Of course it doesn't work. We are supposed to work it."

– Alexander Woollcott, critic (1887-1943)

A university faculty member once quipped, "I believe our students hear in the classroom about organizations of tomorrow and walk out into the world about them and see organizations of yesterday!" Despite societal changes in America that have dramatically impacted our personal and organizational lives, some decision makers still approach problem solving in a very narrow or closed way, irrespective of looking first to the general context in which they must work. Some local officials argue there is only one best way to resolve issues, while others react to problems by trying to balance good and bad consequences in the short term. Still others use some form of personal litmus test to guide their decisions. Unfortunately, many local governments are victims of their own processes, working within rigid arrangements, thoughts, and habits. This makes it almost impossible to respond to change with alacrity or strongly enough. To change the culture in which cities and towns govern is no easy task. It requires the elimination of antiquated procedures and an examination of existing premises that are core to the community as a whole. Those who govern must convey to the community that they are working in a thoughtful manner to address immediate and long-range issues. The Nike prescriptive to "Just Do It!" probably has validity in the sports world; it is of little value as a format for effective local government.

As an initial step in transforming local governance, it is important to identify most of the changes projected to occur in society in general. The best minds forecast that there will be major personal, work, and group adjustments; technological innovations will continue to grow rapidly and in newer dimensions; there will be substantial growth in numbers and activities of government at all levels; and demographic changes will continue to alter the makeup of cities and towns.

Major Personal, Work, and Group Adjustments

It is not surprising that the magnitude and rapidity of population growth has affected local governments in such areas as zoning, planning, and financing. Population growth also has spin-off consequences that once were not as significant as they are today. These spin-offs are now integral components of what once were fairly straightforward areas of decision making. Growth within city and town limits may have sociological impacts that require balancing the public's desires for open space and a sense of neighborhood identification with the need to address issues on an area-wide basis.

Related but not separate adjustments involve an understanding of the changing work ethic that has accompanied population growth. Historically, one could define the American work ethic as traditional – work was a basic value in and of itself whereby people (primarily men) entered the work force at a lower level with the expectation they would move up an organizational ladder (usually in one company) and be rewarded with wages or salary and the title of the position. More recently, however, many workers view the job challenge as the reason for working and remaining with an organization. In short, as long as the challenge exists the employee will be satisfied and remain with the organization. Once the challenge is gone, chances are he or she will look for another place to work. Similarly, more workers now seek employment that allows time and resources to pursue other activities and goals. Many private and public employers fail to recognize and adapt to changing types of work ethics.

The different types of work ethics affect how people interact with city government. Greater freedom from employment obligations gives people more time to engage in community and political activities. Arrangements such as flextime and working from home create more opportunities to observe one's local government and become involved in issues, join community groups, or run for office.

The behavior of groups also has changed. There is less reliance on formal, permanent organizations to achieve goals because communications technology has made it so easy to form ad hoc groups to address single issues. It is not unusual in many communities for individuals to belong to a variety of ad hoc groups and not belong on any continued basis to a formal group. How city councils anticipate and respond to group action is one of the biggest challenges in local government.

As city and town councils struggle to serve their communities, it becomes increasingly necessary for them to factor in the social changes that should impact their decisions. An outside-in council culture requires that council members comprehend the changing nature of the population within their communities and in surrounding areas, as well.

RAPIDLY CHANGING TECHNOLOGICAL DIMENSIONS

The technological revolution has had such dramatic impacts on the individual, the family, education, and government that it is next to impossible to adequately put it into perspective. The spin-off dimensions of technology continue to change how governments in general – and local governments in particular – operate. Technology affects how decisions are made, how functions are carried out, and how the community at large is involved in governance.

Consider a short list of recent advances in technology: faxes, blogging, BlackBerries, televised meetings, text messaging, e-mail, cell phones, high-speed and higher-speed computers, Googling, online purchasing, and economic forecasting. Each has had a phenomenal impact on our lives. Communication tools are invented and marketed at such a fast pace that some devices are considered obsolete almost as soon as they are produced. We have no choice but to accept and use technological innovations as integral parts of doing business, living, and communicating.

One fundamental issue local governments must face is the degree to which technology can enhance or hinder the task of governing. There is little doubt technology has improved the day-to-day administration of cities and towns, especially in crime prevention and policing in general, public works, and the movement to a paperless management system. There is general concern, however, that technology in and of itself may dilute or stifle some aspects of local government, possibly resulting in perverse outcomes. Cities and towns, even small ones, have tried to use technology to improve communications between those in government and the public. But there is often a disconnect between the use of technology and its success in improving communication. How do local governments determine whether the communication technology actually leads to a successful listening audience? A city administrator reported that his government purchased and used state-of-the-art technology designed to communicate with the community faster, more lucidly, more accurately, and in a manner more responsive to current issues and problems. Despite a concerted effort to demonstrate responsiveness on the part of the government, the administrator concluded that there seemed to be less, not more, interest in what the city was doing. But he couldn't know for sure. In his words,

"We have made better communication a major priority in our town so that the public knows what the city is doing and so that they will be able to offer input to the council and administration. The use of modern technology allows us to communicate quickly and in a professional manner; the downside is that we aren't able to accurately determine if anyone is really listening and absorbing what we say, and furthermore we don't really know if we are much further ahead now than in previous attempts to communicate." One could argue that information overload may actually result in diminished levels of face-to-face communications with elected and appointed officials, thereby reinforcing negative views of what government is doing.

There are numerous issues surrounding the impact of technology on how city governments conduct business. Under many open-records laws, all correspondence by regular mail or e-mail is legally public property. While so-called "sunshine laws" restrict face-to-face meetings of two or more members of council to discuss government issues, the same laws apply in the use of e-mails. Communication through e-mail is a matter of public record and other forms of communication between public officials is subject to public scrutiny and exposure, as well. The days of smoke-filled rooms and behind-the-scenes politics definitely belong to a past age.

Here is another unintended consequence of increased technology for local governments: It often leaves little room for pure emotion-attached decisions. Because it is easier than ever to retrieve reliable data in small or large quantities, data often serve as the sole basis for recommending a particular course of action, devoid of public sentiment. An observer of local governments called this "the inter-ocular traumatic test – the message of the data is hitting you right between the eyes!" The downside of relying solely on hard data in decision making is that some conclude there is only one right decision, disregarding either emotion-laden, historical, or value judgments as having validity in supporting or arguing against an issue.

Technology impacts young and old and alters not only how information is discovered but how it is used. Educator Michael Zastrocky has observed that "digital natives," the generation that has grown up with computers and the Internet, are able to engage in multitasking – doing a variety of technological actions, such as e-mailing and text messaging, simultaneously. He and others have observed that this phenomenon might be better described as "multiplexing" because small bits of information are received. This may cause people to focus less on long-term problems and issues. Dr. Zastrocky is of the opinion that many in the younger generation shy away from long-term problem solving and that may be one reason it is difficult for cities and towns to communicate in-depth analyses of local issues.

Substantial Growth in Numbers and Activities of Governments

There are nearly 90,000 units of government in the United States, ranging from special districts to Congress, competing for the same resources at the same time. This phenomenon has resulted in a proliferation of laws, court cases, intergovernmental competition, and a host of mandates and compliance issues. Some argue that this is simply the price we pay for population growth and the needs and wants of society. Others counter that we must amend, repeal, restructure, or simply accommodate to the best of our abilities. Underlying much of this dichotomy are ideological and deep-seated political views held by the many varied segments of the public.

Population growth, geographic shifts, newly incorporated communities, defensive annexations, and the formation of special districts are just part of today's urban landscape. It is not uncommon to find cities or towns whose incorporated boundaries are surrounded – they are, for all intents and purposes, land locked. In such situations the focus of city and town councils is necessarily consumed by this fact and that affects other concerns, including adequate revenue sources, planning and zoning options, and public works services. Ancillary issues such as public schools, open space acquisition, and redevelopment proposals place additional burdens on city and town councils. Options for resolving problems related to the geographic location of a community may be limited to intergovernmental agreements or, in some cases, attempts to form new levels of government. In 1998, for example, the city of Broomfield, Colorado, became a city-county government primarily because the city was located in the corners of four counties. This process was arduous because the Colorado Constitution stipulates that such mergers receive statewide voter approval. Experiments involving large metropolitan governance – such as in Miami-Dade County, Florida – have not met with widespread acceptance.

The delivery of mandated and optional city services is influenced by what the public wants and expects. Some communities want it all – amenities such as recreation centers, hiking trails, and public open spaces *plus* lower taxes, increased service levels, and a sense of local control of their future. At some point, these and other wants conflict and locally elected officials are expected to make difficult choices. State and federal constitutional provisions, mandates, statutory requirements, charter prohibitions, and court decisions are part of what local officials must consider. Some communities have tried other ways to address the wants and needs of constituencies – usually single purpose in nature – such as the formation of cultural, transportation, or recreational districts where revenue is earmarked solely for that purpose. While many of these solutions have been successful, they have fueled the proliferation of government activities. There is often no clear distinction in the mind of a citizen as to who provides what services. This does not mean taxpayers ignore the total amount of tax dollars they pay to live in a community. All too often, however, exactly how much they pay for specific services or benefits is not clearly understood. A council member discussing these issues was quoted as saying, "People need to get real about what we go through to make government work while at the same time we have to protect the public's backsides. That is the reality of city government!" The reality is that tax dollars are spread out over many jurisdictions and pay for a variety of services.

Another result of the omnipresence of government is the growth in lawmaking itself. City council agendas have, by and large, become filled with action items requiring approval or disapproval, many the result of everyday city business. To the casual observer it might appear that the items are not connected in any way or they have not been thoroughly reviewed and debated. Councils frequently are perceived as rubber stamping recommendations or not diligently devoting time to issues at hand. In some instances the latter is true simply because formal approval of small items is required by law. In short, a great amount of "lawmaking" is affirming what is mandated and often non-controversial in content. At the other extreme are council items that do require and deserve extended review and debate, and those may be indirectly connected to other local issues. Council members in these instances are faced with the thorny task of reaching a decision that may set an entirely new policy direction. Studies show that in council-manager cities, councils approve about 90 percent of agenda items recommended by the administration. The other 10 percent, as one might suspect, are usually the most contentious or troublesome in nature.

An interesting change in the governmental role of making law is what appears to be a reversal in why laws are enacted in the first place. Historically, laws were enacted to prohibit activities contrary to the public good, usually accompanied by prescribed penalties of some kind. The changing nature of society and its perception of the role of government have led to the passage of laws that permit, rather than prohibit, various activities. Examples are laws that allow breast feeding in public or let motorists turn left on a red light from a one-way street to another one-way street. Lobbying by public and special-interest groups for legislation to allow certain activities is opposite from the historical pressures on lawmakers to prevent some activities from taking place. The demands on councils, as at other levels of government, will in all likelihood continue to be that of wanting laws that permit rather than prohibit. The adage "There ought to be law!" still holds true.

Despite some oratory to the contrary, there likely will be more pressure on governments to find immediate solutions to problems. There will be calls for changes in how local governments are organized, but it is more likely there will be growth in public action groups that want council decisions on a case-by-case basis. Multi-membership in existing interest groups and ad hoc groups undoubtedly will continue to grow. It is not uncommon, for example, for individuals to belong to any number of groups whose missions on the surface may appear to contradict one another – perhaps the Sierra Club, Citizens for Prairie Dog Relocation, the Ad Hoc Committee for Street Widening, and the Chamber of Commerce. Additionally, a group sometimes changes its mission in an effort to increase the number of active participants. City and town councils that in their zeal ask for more citizen involvement should be prepared for increased interest and scrutiny by the public in how the city is governed. Through technology, groups can share knowledge about issues without ever holding face-to-face meetings.

Citizen involvement in governmental matters will continue to increase under the general umbrella of direct democracy. The growing use of initiatives, referenda, and recall elections has afforded greater citizen participation, especially in states and local communities. The mere threat by citizens to petition for a recall election may trigger other actions that may serve to satisfy the goals of petitioners. The referendum option can set forth policy alternatives for ratification or defeat. The initiative allows citizens to essentially enact public policy or it gives them a means of objecting to a particular policy. Each form of direct democracy involves public expenditures for holding elections and each may generate considerable media attention. At times councils have used initiatives and referenda to seek public approval or disapproval on any number of issues on which they cannot agree or to place the decision-making burden on the shoulders of voters.

Demographic Changes

Demographic changes impact cities and towns in many ways. The national debate about legal and illegal immigration is a major political issue affecting both urban and rural communities. While immigration laws have been for the most part a federal concern, the illegal immigration debate is growing in cities, towns, and state legislatures. Some municipalities, for example, have labeled themselves "sanctuary cities" in which ordinances prohibit city police and employees from asking people about their immigration status. It is unlikely that the disagreements over immigration will be resolved anytime soon. Expect conflicts that surface over proposed solutions to be intense.

Population growth by itself has changed how cities and towns make decisions. Since 1850 the U.S. population has increased more than 1,000 percent and the consequences of population growth have created numerous problems for city and town councils. Citizen demands for slow growth or no growth have created spin-off issues that councils must confront. Environmentalist groups, for example, have called for more mass transit options, the purchase of open space, and strict regulation of housing and commercial developments. These issues necessarily require economic decisions and have sociological consequences, as well. Sprawl, which devoured desert land in metropolitan Phoenix at the rate of an acre an hour in the 1990s, affects quality-of-life issues in both large and small cities. The rate and magnitude of small-city sprawl may not be comparable to that of Phoenix or Atlanta, but the issues are just as real. The differences between large urban areas and small communities on this matter are more likely differences of degree rather than of kind.

Immigration and population growth continue to change the ethnic composition of the United States, where approximately 80 percent of immigrants are from Asia and Latin America. Minorities, people who are other than single-race non-Hispanic whites, made up one-third of the U.S. population in 2006. By 2050, minorities are expected to constitute one-half of the population, and nearly one in five Americans will have been born outside of the country. Since 1980 the Asian-American and Hispanic populations have more than tripled, Native Americans have nearly doubled in size as a group, and the African-American population is up nearly 50 percent. The growing numbers of minorities and immigrants requires local governments to adopt multi-cultural approaches to many community issues.

Demographic changes also are dramatically evident when looking at age and its impact on workforce development. The number of older workers in the United States is growing much faster than the overall labor pool. People 25 to 54 —those of prime working age – are expected to make up 64 percent of the civilian workforce in 2050, down from 71 percent in 2000. People 65 and older are projected to constitute more than 7 percent of the workforce in 2050, up from 3 percent in 2000.

Demographic changes will play a major role in determining how citizens expect councils to make decisions on such matters as residential and commercial developments, land-use planning, cultural and recreational enhancements, and environmental management. Tasks that once were relatively easy to handle, based primarily upon economic capability, must now be assessed in the context of demographic change. Items on council agendas may appear straightforward, but more than likely there are numerous implicit, if not explicit, issues to be considered before a decision is reached. As has been pointed out numerous times in many council chambers, the simpler the issue and the fewer dollars involved, the longer the debate and more complex the decision process becomes. The reverse seems also to be true – complicated and highly expensive issues seem to generate shorter discussions and more expedited decision making.

There are, of course, many outside-in factors that reflect the changing nature of our culture and they all affect how city and town councils behave one way or another. The factors discussed in this section, however, are of such significance that they generally permeate most actions in city halls and seem to be growing in impact exponentially. These and other factors affect different cities and towns in different ways, depending on population size, geographic location, and history. The issue, however, is not *if* these factors will affect local government but *when* and to what degree. Citizen demands for creative leadership in communities will increase in new and different ways, and those who assume leadership roles will have as their biggest challenge that of formulating a new and different leadership paradigm at city hall.

THE NEED FOR NEW AND DIFFERENT LEADERSHIP PARADIGMS

"These are the times in which a genius would wish to live. It is not in the still calm of life…that great characters are formed. The habits of a vigorous mind are formed in contending with difficulties. Great necessities call out great virtues."

– Abigail Adams, 1780

The quip "take me to your leader" may never be more appropriate in local government as now, when communities have greater expectations from city and town officials. Those elected and appointed to local offices serve as representatives of many constituencies and are generally perceived as local political leaders. Much of what local governments do are the traditional functions within their legal purview. Those in office are expected to carry out their legal duties with honesty and integrity. But the changing nature of society has added an extra obligation, a personal or group expectation of leadership, often not explicitly defined nor clearly articulated.

The word *leadership* did not appear in literature until the 19th century and since then there have been as many definitions of the term as definers. History books often designate people as leaders by their successes in public office or private enterprise – for example, George Washington, Abraham Lincoln, and Andrew Carnegie. Others have attempted to itemize personal traits that, when put together in some type of taxonomy, describe a leader as opposed to a non-leader. Most students of the subject agree that leaders are not born; they are made. Moreover, time, circumstances, and probably a great amount of luck have a lot to do with whether one is perceived as a leader.

Defining leadership and identifying leaders is not unlike the judicial attempt to define pornography – "I know it when I see it." Conversely, in local politics and, indeed, in all politics, a void in leadership and leader capabilities is quickly discerned by the public.

Although leadership may be a nebulous concept, citizens expect that those elected to a city council will be leaders. It is difficult to generalize about council leaders given the number and diversity of council members across the country. In some communities, individuals labeled as leaders receive numerous accolades and honors for their service. In other communities, council members receive a minimum of congratulations for work accomplished in their time of office. Almost all council members, at one time or another, receive a plaque or certificate of appreciation for serving on the council. Some truly have been leaders while others have dutifully fulfilled what one authority labeled as a "clerkship" role. The identified leaders were those who carried out their clerkship duties and showed an ability to persuade and influence others. Thus, the ability to persuade and influence sets some apart from others. The true leaders often look to the future beyond the tasks of today.

A Typology of Council Leaders

It might be helpful to establish a classification of council members in order to clarify the leadership issue. As mentioned earlier, there are no definite and established reasons that motivate people to run for election to a city council. A normative classification, however, might help define leadership styles.

Generally, one can identify three types of council member behaviors that also may help explain their motivations for seeking office: the Negativist, the Positivist, and the Hybrid.

The Negativist is a very popular candidate in American cities and towns. He or she has as a primary campaign theme one or more issues that are negative in content, such as opposition to an annexation, opposition to planning and development proposals, or criticism of how policies are administered. Candidates who speak in negative terms about policies are very popular with voters. One should not assume that the Negativist is without reasons for his or her positions, and one should assume that the Negativist may emerge as the most popular candidate running for office. Unfortunately, the Negativist, once elected, also assumes that his or her victory was due to the negativism of the campaign, and he or she carries that theme into making many, if not most, decisions at the council table. In sum, the Negativist has a kind of tunnel vision and argues and votes on every issue from his or her perceived voter mandate to be a negative force on the council. There is very little room for compromise in the Negativist's view of leadership. No matter the issue, the Negativist looks for some reason to vote "no."

The Positivist is also a very popular candidate who focuses on themes requiring active, rather than reactive, actions by the city council. Themes such as protecting the environment, limiting population growth and sprawl, and purchasing open space are common and resonate with many voters. The Positivist, much like the Negativist, may also be guilty of a type of tunnel vision that he or she believes is a result of a voter mandate. Positivists, like Negativists, are passionate about the themes that they perceive led to their election victory and incorporate them into their decision making. Positivists often analyze issues based on how they relate to the positive theme or themes of their campaign, and they will approve or disapprove policies that incorporate or ignore those themes, respectively. The Positivist can usually be counted on to vote "yes" on those items that in some way embed his or her themes, even tangentially, in the topic. The converse is equally true – count on a "no" vote or little participation in debate if the themes are not obviously germane in the eyes of the Positivist to the issue at hand. The Positivist is usually an optimistic person who avoids proposing or participating in issues that might lead to disharmony on the council.

Both Negativists and Positivists believe that acceptance of their leadership rests in how well they incorporate their campaign positions into actions brought before the council. Extreme Negativists and Positivists are highly predictable in how they approach issues in their roles as elected representatives. In many instances both are solid, well-intentioned members of council who often seek re-election and are successful in doing so. Both are prominently visible to the media and the community at large. But both, because of their commitment to positions taken before their elections, may cause councils to become bogged down in irrelevant discussions and dilatory decision making. This can lead to public dissatisfaction with a city council. Negativists and Positivists often believe that in order to fulfill their representative roles they must be consistent in how they approach and vote on all issues. Consistency sometimes becomes more of a basis for their support or opposition to issues rather than the substantive merit of those issues.

The third type of behavior can be described as the Hybrid. Upon seeking office, he or she cannot be defined as a Positivist or Negativist but may have shared some, but not all, of their views. The Hybrid has the most difficult role once elected for a couple of reasons. He or she is likely to be accused of not always being consistent in voting or addressing issues. Some may label the Hybrid as a "flip-flopper," but in reality the Hybrid takes each issue or problem as it emerges. His or her position is formed around circumstances, events, and facts. In a very real sense, the Hybrid has the most difficult task because he or she is not predictable. The Hybrid is not the equivalent of a devil's advocate, although others may view him or her that way. Rather, Hybrids seek to maintain an open mind before making decisions and, in so doing, they will reach conclusions that to them are correct given each situation. Hybrids are frequently frustrated with their experiences on the council and often forego re-election.

There are probably other leadership styles one could attach to various members of councils but the Negativist, Positivist, and Hybrid incorporate the majority of them. The real issue is the degree to which these leadership styles hinder effective city government. The Negativist and Positivist both suffer from being single-purposed in their approaches to decision making but, depending upon the issue at hand, they might very well be effective leaders. In other words, the issue may call for a definite Positivist or Negativist position. The Hybrid, on the other hand, is always looking for the best possible solution to an issue based on many factors. The Hybrid might share some opinions with the Negativist or Positivist, but reach a different conclusion on the same issue. The Hybrid's concept of leadership is pragmatic and situational. He or she is not constrained to support or reject an issue because of any single view of local government. Given the complexity of local government issues and problems, the Hybrid is the most preferred style of leadership but the most difficult to fulfill.

THE LEADERSHIP PARADIGM SHIFT

The societal changes previously noted – in personal and group dynamics, the work ethic, technology, government activities, and demographics – are directly or indirectly changing the leadership paradigm for local governments. At the very least, they are shifting the paradigm ingredients to the extent that leaders must embrace new modes of addressing issues. There is no single formula for leadership, and certainly a "one size fits all" approach is dangerous if not futile. Each city and town council will need to work as a unit to examine the leadership paradigm shifts that impact the behavior of members as elected representatives. This is not an easy task; it requires an in-depth, definitive assessment of leadership roles. While the Duke of Wellington asked his lieutenants to be "brave" and Napoleon wanted generals who were "lucky," these qualities by themselves are not enough to fight city hall battles in the 21st century. There is no scientific recipe that will assure a successful outcome in all circumstances. It is useful to recall that Lewis Carroll began his career by writing about algebra and geometry but concluded his pursuit of understanding the world by writing *Alice's Adventures in Wonderland* and *Through the Looking Glass*. The paradigm shift will require councils to use a mixture of hard and reliable data, emotion, and a good amount of fanciful design.

The leadership paradigm shift means that councils will have to adopt an outside-in culture as they conduct city business. As noted earlier, this phenomenon suggests that councils will need to discard unnecessary procedures, processes, and structures while questioning their basic premises for making decisions. This change does not negate the usefulness of vision statements, goal setting, or strategic planning. It requires, however, that such long-term commitments begin with a working knowledge of cultural variables that will affect their constituencies. This is no small undertaking; it requires looking outside first before making inside decisions. It means that leadership must be viewed as a shared function wherein each member of council has a role, irrespective of title, length of tenure, or any real or perceived mandates from voters. Negativists, Positivists, and Hybrids will each have to make political and personal adjustments in the way thorny as well as mundane issues are handled. People elected to city councils must adopt renaissance leadership characteristics if local governments are to be more effective.

THE CHARACTERISTICS AND TRAITS OF A 21ST CENTURY RENAISSANCE LEADER

The term *renaissance* has been applied to the methods of European learning between the 14th and 17th centuries, when scholars revived the ideas of Roman and Greek thinkers and applied them to contemporary governments. It is not suggested here that this is the case in the 21st century, although much can be gleaned from the Greeks and Romans in their views about society and governing. Rather, a more useful connotation might include the definitions of *generalist* or *multidisciplinary* in assessing a wide variety of views, issues, events, problems, trends, and knowledge as bases for problem solving. This suggests avoiding narrow views of topics and assuming that solutions to problems in local government are not always apparent or reducible to simplistic terms or equations. In 21st century local government, council leaders will need to consciously exhibit renaissance characteristics as they make decisions.

The renaissance leader is always on a learning curve, struggling internally to reconcile in a rational way whether adopted goals should remain static even though circumstances change. In his 1970 book *Future Shock*, Alvin Toffler wrote that one of our problems is not that we lack goals but that we are faced with resolving or choosing between conflicting goals. Renaissance leaders do not abandon goals; they manage conflicting goals and eschew consistency. Changing one's mind is often met with severe criticism. But goals can be viewed as hypotheses that are continually under scrutiny and can be discarded for new and even better-working hypotheses. The renaissance leader in local government seeks ways to challenge – and persuade others to challenge – established goals and learns how to manage those that conflict with one another. This means the leader is required to look for credible forecasts about future events.

The issues of power and authority also confront the renaissance leader. If authority comes with the office – meaning it is spelled out in statute, ordinance, or charter – it is relatively easy to determine what authority is bestowed on a city council, mayor, or city administrator. Power, however, is an ambiguous term, and some city councils believe that authority is synonymous with power. It is not. As noted earlier, power involves the ability to persuade and influence and is not necessarily ascribed to any single person or office. The renaissance leader believes power is a positive force that should consciously be used to address the issue at hand and not be used the same way in every circumstance. Some may argue that the use of power is a negative approach to problem solving in local government. Leaders, however, do not embrace insidious methods and must be skillful in persuasion. Renaissance leaders will learn to observe sociologist Louis Wirth's comment that "The Chinese … are reported to have a way of writing the word *crisis* by two characters, one of which signifies danger, the other opportunity." Finally, as Greek historian Thucydides (460 B.C. -395 B.C.) observed, the restraint of power may make a more immediate and lasting impression than anything.

Although authority and power are integral parts of council behavior, they are not sufficient as the only variables for renaissance leadership. The renaissance leader must also learn to anticipate what might or might not occur, and that presumes he or she will have some type of vision of reality. In the 1880s and 1890s, Woodrow Wilson had not yet been elected president, but he wrote numerous essays on leadership and administration. Wilson argued that successful leaders were those who could "read the common thought" and "interpret." For renaissance council members, this means trying to anticipate the mood of the public, predict what events could occur either positively or negatively, and figure out what steps could be taken in anticipation of future developments in the life of the community.

Not all issues and problems brought before a city council lead to major differences of opinion, but there are a sufficient number of cases that generate heated debates and sometimes divisiveness among members. The renaissance leader learns to fight by appointment, choosing which situations require argument and persuasion and which are better left alone. Sometimes, as it is said, it is better to win the peace than the war. Many factors should be considered by the renaissance leader to determine when to engage in battle. And just as battles should not be fought on every issue or problem, the renaissance leader should know when a battle is over, when there is nothing more to be stated that will lead to a conclusion that he or she wants. In these circumstances the renaissance leader, to paraphrase scripture, can sense that additional arguments will not change anyone's mind and he or she should shake the dust off one's sandals and move on.

Unfortunately, many believe that a final vote on a matter is conclusive enough to show that democracy is working. But voting either by majority rule or plurality is not the same as consensus. True, the voting process allows a count of "ayes" and "nays" on a matter, but that does not assure everyone had an opportunity to share in the reasoning for a vote. Consensus building takes time and leadership that tries to assure that, when a final tally is taken, everyone has had an opportunity to participate equally in the process. Moreover, split votes may end debate but there may be no clear guidelines for those who are to administer outcomes. Democracy was at work, but the reasons for a "no" or "yes" vote may not have been fully or freely discussed. The renaissance leader plays a role in asking for all opinions and views on an issue before a vote is taken. In the 1600s English philosopher John Locke argued that taking votes was civilized and better than bashing heads together to determine outcomes. Consensus building should be a high priority of the renaissance leader before voting takes place.

The renaissance leader is continually looking beyond the immediate and imagining how future events will affect today's decisions. This role is not that of a prophet so much as it is having the ability to put decisions into an outside-in framework that realistically depicts the nature of local government. Imagine a giant, swinging pendulum that moves swiftly or slowly from one extreme – the freedom to address community issues – to a position on the other end that restricts these factors. The renaissance leader has the task of persuading others to keep the pendulum from behaving erratically. This task has both short- and long-term implications and, in essence, it means the renaissance leader is helping the city avoid or minimize erratic consequences. A member of a council once erroneously opined that he believed his primary responsibility was "dedication to immediate problem solving, and future councils would have the authority to make any necessary changes under circumstances that exist at that time." All forecasts about future changes do not allow the luxury of such an approach to local governance.

The renaissance leader makes mistakes, sometimes in judgment and sometimes in his or her zeal to be well versed in a variety of topics facing a council. These may be avoided, to some degree, by being secure in one's ability to make clear distinctions along different dimensions – the ability to distinguish between efficiency and effectiveness, between artifacts of political life and the intrinsic behavior patterns of human behavior, between means and ends, and between a view of disparate parts of community wishes and needs and that of the common good. The renaissance leader is not a saint; he or she is one who has formed a philosophy of local government, is able to balance happiness and anger, and can articulate his or her core values of life in general and government in particular. The renaissance leader is engaged in life-long learning and is continually examining his or her perspectives and in what ways they can be improved and, if necessary, altered. Renaissance leaders subscribe to the provisions of the Athenian Oath, striving to "… transmit this City, not only not less, but greater and more beautiful than it was transmitted to us."

The characteristics of the renaissance leader must include, above all, the ability to translate his or her views, philosophy, values, and concerns into the daily role of being a representative. Indeed, this assumes that the leader has formulated a philosophy of representative government. He or she believes that those elected to city councils have a greater role than serving as mere delegates. Rather, council representatives are trustees (thus the name frequently given to town council members) and as trustees they owe, in the words of John F. Kennedy, a first responsibility to their own consciences rather than to political parties or even constituencies. Renaissance leaders base their actions on this underlying premise of representative government and from that foundation they use various leadership talents, skills, and conscious choices in solving problems and making decisions on the city council.

CONCLUSION

Representative government is, by all definitions and perspectives, complex and necessary if democracy is to function. Local governance, that which is closest to the people, is exciting, demanding, and important for the common good. Those elected to local offices have many roles to play and, unlike most of the private sector, there are many constraints on how these roles are carried out. The public is not comparable to the stockholders of private corporations, even though local councils often hear a chant that "Our town should be run like a business." And while there are some business-sector practices that can be borrowed for use by a city or town, the overall framework and the so-called "bottom line" simply is not the same. The common good or the public interest is greater than the sum of the parts; it is fluid and it has energy of its own. For the most part, those elected to city and town councils are thrust into environments with firmly established legal and non-legal barriers that inhibit or restrict decision making. Local governance is conducted in a political arena that requires men and women to play by the rules while at the same time they are expected to be innovative, creative, and bold in directing the affairs of the community. Determining at any one time what is the public interest is a more complex process than simply adding up individual interests to reach a comprehensive definition. The political environment assumes that those elected have in their own minds what constitutes the public interest.

Given the changing dynamics of society and the nature of 21st century politics, it is incumbent upon those in governing roles to become renaissance leaders. As noted earlier, leaders are made, not born. It is highly unlikely that new or radically different forms of local government will be invented. But it is likely that the nature of the populace will change in many ways and those changes will have an even greater impact than at present. Still, those in representative roles will be expected to not only continue to oversee the provision of historic municipal services at high levels of quality, but also keep budgets balanced and minimize the imposition of additional financial burdens. It is a universal equation with no single correct answer for each city and town. The apparent option is for elected representatives to assume new leadership traits in order for a community to survive and survive well. In short, the outside-in focus will require a change in how individuals carry out their leadership roles. Clearly, this will not be the panacea for handling all local government problems and issues. However, the failure to change the leadership paradigm increases the chances for greater community dissatisfaction coupled with a status quo syndrome pervading the council's approach to governing.

More than 70 years ago, in the landmark book *Politics: Who Gets What, When, How*, political scientist Harold Lasswell set forth the need to understand governmental organizations contextually. In non-academic terms, Lasswell meant that you cannot fully understand government apart from politics. In addition, Lasswell described five questions that are relevant in all political situations and are applicable today and for the future of local government. His questions about goals, trends, conditions, future projections, and alternatives are the essence of the renaissance leader's thinking as he or she leads and makes decisions. The framework suggests that renaissance leaders focus first on the context in which they are carrying out their representative roles before making decisions. This also means that a leader's ideological or personally held partisan positions should be put aside before reaching a position.

But renaissance leaders are not so naïve or parochial as to believe that ideology and partisanship will not arise and become even a small part of a decision-making process. The difference between the renaissance leader and others is that he or she does not make partisanship or ideology the premise for decision making. Rather, the leader anticipates the possibility that issues can surface at any time. The renaissance leader, like Sir Thomas More in *A Man for All Seasons*, is viewed as a person of principle who can be relied upon to take his or her role seriously, with due diligence to homework. And when an issue is resolved, he or she can assume a leadership role in addressing new issues and problems, absent ideological or personal biases but always with a focused and integrative approach as an elected representative of the community.

The views and assumptions in this book are, of course, my own and while others over the years have contributed to my perspectives on local government and leadership, they would not necessarily claim ownership of them. My words here are from working with city and town councils, teaching undergraduate and graduate students, conducting research, engaging in professional workshops and institutes, serving in elective and appointive offices, and in spending considerable time in my career thinking about how important local government is to a democratic society. Leadership, that elusive word, is still the most central concept that society clamors for, and local government must assume that role. If all predictions for our future come true, it will be even more imperative that city and town councils be the level of government where leadership is required. Managing and resolving issues will remain the responsibility of local governance. Leadership will remain the chief responsibility of city and town councils. When asked, "Who's Running This Town, Anyway?" the question will need to include a concurrent query, "How is This Town Being Led?"

TITLES FOR THE BOOKSHELF OF EVERY LOCAL OFFICIAL

It is presumptuous for anyone to tell others what books, papers, manuscripts, or documents ought to be in their personal or professional libraries. I am only suggesting here what I believe are just a few bookshelf items that local government officials should possess and read. As a graduate student, one of my mentors told me to never place a book on my bookshelf that I have not read. For many years I have said the same thing to my students and, true to my mentor, I have tried to follow his advice. Needless to say, the floor in my study is stacked high with books and documents.

The field of local government is ripe with documentation and, obviously, what should be acquired or required reading is pretty much a subjective opinion. But certain works should be read and yes, even reread, to refresh one's mind about various topics that bear on local government. To be very subjective, there simply are valued works that belong on one's local government bookshelf much like the acquisitions of those who are fly fishers or golfers. At a minimum the latter would have a copy of Norman Maclean's *A River Runs Through It and Other Stories* and Ben Hogan's *Five Lessons: The Modern Fundamentals of Golf.* In these subject areas there is, of course, an abundance of publications. But at some point, one makes a choice as to what belongs on a shelf and what is appropriately stacked neatly on the floor along with the numerous items in the same categories. These should not be discarded. Rather, until read they should remain in one's possession as part of a life-long learning venture and then shelved with the others.

I have listed some items that I believe can serve as a beginning to a library collection. They are not in a specific chronological order or in a subject-matter category. I am confident that, much like fly fishing or golf aficionados, a large local government library can easily be created.

The List:

Plato, *The Republic*

Your state constitution

Your city charter and council bylaws

Aristotle, *Politics*

Robert's Rules of Order

Lincoln Steffens, *The Shame of the Cities*

Tom Cronin, *Direct Democracy*

Richard S. Childs, *Civic Victories*

Niccolo Machiavelli, *The Prince*

Woodrow Wilson, *The Study of Administration*

Patrick Lencioni, *The Five Dysfunctions of a Team: A Leadership Fable*

Harold Lasswell, *Politics: Who Gets What, When, How*

Robert Caro, *The Power Broker: Robert Moses and the Fall of New York*

Louis Brownlow, *A Passion for Anonymity*

John F. Kennedy, *Profiles in Courage*

Thomas Paine, *Common Sense and the Crisis*

Jim Collins, *Good to Great*

Alexis de Tocqueville, *Democracy in America*

Henri Pirenne, *Medieval Cities*

Richard E. Neustadt, *Presidential Power: The Politics of Leadership*

Kenneth Blanchard, *The One Minute Manager*

The Athenian Oath (suitable for framing)

Ritchie P. Lowry, *Who's Running This Town? Community Leadership and Social Change*

ABOUT THE AUTHOR

Dr. John C. Buechner is President Emeritus of the University of Colorado and Professor Emeritus of the School of Public Affairs. He has held a variety of university administrative positions including Associate Dean of Arts and Sciences and Chancellor of the University of Colorado at Denver, Assistant to the President of the University for Governmental Relations, and Director of the Bureau of Government Research and Service. During his 40-plus years at the university he has taught undergraduate and graduate courses in local and state government, public administration, and American government.

Dr. Buechner received his B.A. in political science from The College of Wooster and his M.P.A. and Ph.D. from the University of Michigan.

In addition to his academic career, Dr. Buechner also served his community as a member of the Board of Zoning Adjustment, Planning Commission, twice elected to the City Council, mayor pro tempore, and mayor of the city of Boulder, Colorado. He was elected to the Colorado House of Representatives and ran for Congress.

He has authored or co-authored four books, numerous articles, and monographs and has served on numerous civic and governmental boards and commissions. He has been a consultant to more than 35 local governments and other agencies and has received numerous awards and honors for his contributions to state and local governments.

Dr. Buechner resides in Lafayette, Colorado.

PROPERTY OF THE CITY
OF MARYLAND HEIGHTS